BALTI *Spice* RECIPES

PARRAGON

BALTI

Spice

RECIPES

Exotic Dishes Flavoured with Spices

First published in Great Britain in 1996 by
Parragon Book Service Ltd
Unit 13-17, Avonbridge Trading Estate
Atlantic Road, Avonmouth
Bristol BS11 9QD

ISBN: 0-7525-1974-3

Printed in the United Kingdom

Produced by Kingfisher Design, London

Acknowledgements
Series Design: Pedro Prá-Lopez, Kingfisher Design, London
Designers: Frank Landamore, Frances Prá-Lopez, Kingfisher Design, London
Series Editor: Diana Vowles
Illustrations: Jill Moore
Photography and Styling: Patrick McLeavey
Home Economist: Jennie Berresford

Material contained in this book has previously appeared in
Balti Cooking

Note
Cup measurements in this book are for American cups.
Tablespoons are assumed to be 15ml.
Unless otherwise stated, milk is assumed to be full-fat,
eggs are standard size 2 and pepper is freshly ground black pepper

Contents

Balti Cooking

alti cooking may be a more recent export from the Indian subcontinent than the ubiquitous curries the West has come to love, but it is catching up fast in terms of popularity. It hails from the mountains of northern Pakistan, and gains its name from the particular type of pot in which it is cooked; the Balti pan is a large, deep, two-handled pot with a rounded bottom, resembling a Chinese wok. 'Balti' means 'cooking bucket', and this down-to-earth name gives a good idea of its sturdy, purposeful nature.

In this area of the world, the influences of India, Pakistan, China, Afghanistan and Iran meet. The technique of stir-frying (and indeed the shape of the pan itself) was probably borrowed from China, while the use of spices is very typical of the Indian subcontinent. In Balti cooking, though, the rice that we traditionally associate with Chinese and Indian food gives way to naan bread and chapatis, used to scoop the meat and sauce direct from the Balti pan.

Because of the brevity of stir-frying, it is best to use good-quality ingredients, cut into bite-sized pieces. Spices such as curry leaves, bay leaves, cloves, cardamom pods and cinnamon sticks are used whole, fried in oil to release their flavour. These should not be eaten, whereas ground spices are absorbed deliciously into the food to contribute to the heady aromas that have featured in Asian food for centuries.

Popular spice ingredients

Paprika, garam masala and mustard seeds are popular spices that appear in many Balti dishes. Paprika, like chilli powder, cayenne pepper, Tabasco sauce and pepper sauce, is a product of the *Capsicum* family, which includes hot chilli peppers as well as sweet

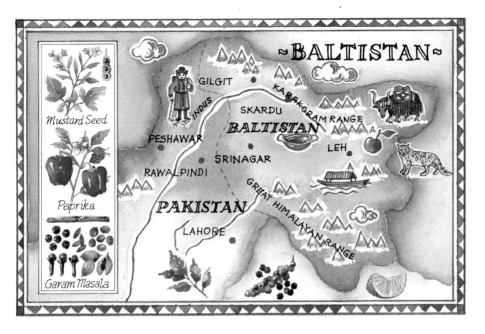

(bell) peppers. Capsicums come from Central and South America and the Caribbean, and had already been cultivated there for thousands of years by the time the Spanish arrived in the 15th century.

While the Spaniards were at first surprised to see the indigenous peoples eating such hot 'fruit', capsicums were soon introduced to Europe and by the 17th century the herbalist John Parkinson was able to describe no fewer than 20 different varieties that were to be seen growing in Italy and Spain. From there they found their way along the Silk Road, which wound its way from China to Rome across terrain that ranged from the Taklamakan Desert, the hottest place on earth, to the mountains of the Hindu Kush. After peppercorns, the capsicum spices are the most important in the spice trade. Today, India is the largest producer and one of the major exporters, along with Japan, China,

Indonesia and Thailand. The chilli harvest lasts about three months, and the chillies are dried either in the sun or artificially before being processed into powders, pastes and sauces.

The secrets of garam masala

Garam masala appears in many dishes from the north of the subcontinent, though there is no such thing as a standard mix! It may consist of just two or three spices, or of twelve; it may be hot and fiery, or it may be gently aromatic. Sometimes the spices are used whole, sometimes they are ground; and for a very grand dish, dried rose petals may add a touch of luxury. The only common element in the use of garam masala is that it is added sparingly.

Mustard has been used for its flavour and also for its medicinal qualities since the days of antiquity – a reference to it has been found in an Egyptian medical document dating from about 1550BC. It was the only spice that was easily affordable in Europe until the end of the fifteenth century, when the Portuguese explorer Vasco da Gama returned from the East bearing exotic spices that were to leave their mark on the European diet. Today, mustard is grown in a large number of temperate countries and the pods must be harvested when they are ripe but before they burst. In Asian cuisine, the seeds are usually heated in hot oil until they begin to pop in order to bring out their flavour.

Par-cooking

Because Balti dishes are stir-fried, tougher cuts of meat such as braising steak have to be par-cooked in advance. Alternatively, you can cook the Balti curry for about 1 hour, preferably in a covered dish in the oven at 180°C/350°F/Gas mark 4.

The sauce from the par-cooked meat can be used to add extra liquid and flavour to other recipes; blend all the ingredients except the meat to a smooth purée in a food processor or blender or push them through a sieve (strainer). So that you will always have some to hand, make double the quantity of sauce when you are following a recipe which uses par-cooked meat and freeze it in small portions to use as required in a recipe or any curry that needs a little extra liquid.

You can make a Balti sauce suitable for vegetarians by omitting the meat from the par-cooked meat recipe, in which case you will need to cook the sauce in the oven or on the hob for 40 minutes. If you don't have any sauce ready, you can use a good stock instead.

Par-cooked lamb or beef

This is the recipe used for the par-cooked meat that appears in the recipes in this book.

1 tbsp oil

250 g / 8 oz / 2 cups chopped onion

2 garlic cloves, crushed

1 tsp ground ginger

1 fresh green chilli, chopped

1 tsp garam masala (see page 22)

1 tbsp tomato purée (paste)

1 tsp salt

½ tsp brown onion seeds

200 ml / 7 fl oz / 1 scant cup water

750 g / 1½ lb braising steak or lamb, cubed

1 Heat the oil in a flameproof casserole, add the onion and fry until softened. Add the garlic and fry for 1 minute.

2 Stir in the remaining ingredients and bring to the boil. Put the lid on the casserole and cook in a preheated oven at 200°C/400°F/Gas mark 6, allowing 40 minutes for lamb and 1 hour for beef. The meat should be tender but still pink in the centre.

3 Remove the meat with a slotted spoon and use the remaining contents of the casserole to make a Balti sauce.

Balti Tiger Prawns (Jumbo Shrimp)

SERVES 4

1 garlic clove, crushed
2 tsp freshly grated ginger root
2 tsp ground coriander
2 tsp ground cumin
½ tsp ground cardamom
¼ tsp chilli powder
2 tbsp tomato purée (paste)
5 tbsp water
3 tbsp chopped fresh coriander (cilantro)
500 g / 1 lb peeled cooked tiger prawns
  (jumbo shrimp)
2 tbsp oil
2 small onions, sliced
1 fresh green chilli, chopped
salt

1 Put the garlic, ginger, ground coriander, cumin, cardamom, chilli powder, tomato purée (paste), 4 tablespoons water and 2 tablespoons fresh coriander (cilantro) into a bowl. Mix all the ingredients together.

2 Add the prawns (shrimp) to the bowl and leave to marinate for 2 hours.

3 Heat the oil in a Balti pan or wok, add the onions and stir-fry until golden brown.

4 Add the prawns (shrimp), marinade and fresh chilli and stir-fry over a medium heat for 5 minutes. Add the salt, and the remaining tablespoon of water if the mixture is very dry. Stir-fry over a medium heat for a further 5 minutes.

5 Serve immediately, sprinkled with the remaining fresh coriander (cilantro).

Green Chilli & Galangal Prawns (Shrimp)

SERVES 4

2 tbsp oil
4 garlic cloves, crushed
2.5 cm / 1 inch fresh galangal root, grated
500 g / 1lb peeled cooked tiger prawns
   (jumbo shrimp)
2 fresh green chillies, sliced
1 tbsp lemon juice
1 tbsp tomato purée (paste)
180 ml / 6 fl oz / ¾ cup coconut milk
¾ tsp garam masala (see page 22)
1 tsp salt
1 tbsp chopped fresh coriander (cilantro)

1 Heat the oil in a Balti pan or wok, add the garlic and galangal and stir-fry until golden brown.

2 Add the prawns (shrimp) and green chillies and stir-fry for 3 minutes.

3 Stir in the lemon juice, tomato purée (paste), coconut milk, garam masala and salt. Simmer for 8–10 minutes until the prawns (shrimp) are cooked.

4 Add the fresh coriander (cilantro) and serve at once.

CHILLIES

Chillies come in many shapes, sizes and degrees of hotness and are usually red or green. These recipes mainly use fresh green chillies, which are generally milder than red chillies. The seeds are the really fiery part, so remove them if you like a milder curry. Dried red chillies are sold whole, crushed or ground. Don't touch your face or eyes while handling fresh chillies as the juices will burn the skin, and wash your hands thoroughly afterwards.

GALANGAL

Galangal is related to ginger and resembles it in appearance, though it has a more peppery taste. It is used chopped or sliced. Galangal will probably only be found in Asian food stores, but ginger root can be used as a substitute.

Deep-fried Battered Fish with Fenugreek Dip

SERVES 4

125 g / 4 oz / 1 cup gram flour or plain
  (all-purpose) flour
2 tsp garam masala (see page 22)
4 tsp brown mustard seeds
2 eggs
1 tbsp oil
120–150 ml / 4–5 fl oz / ½–⅔ cup coconut
  milk
500 g / 1 lb plaice fillets, skinned, and cut
  into 1.5 cm / ½ inch strips
300 ml / ½ pint / 1¼ cups oil for deep-frying
lemon wedges to serve

DIP:
150 ml / ¼ pint / ⅔ cup thick creamy yogurt
2 tbsp chopped fresh fenugreek
½ tsp garam masala (see page 22)
1 tsp tomato purée (paste)

1 Sift the flour into a bowl and add the garam masala and mustard seeds. Make a well in the centre and gradually add the eggs, 1 tablespoon of oil and enough coconut milk to make a batter which has the consistency of thick cream.

2 Coat the strips of fish in the batter and set aside.

3 To make the fenugreek dip, put the yogurt, fenugreek, garam masala and tomato purée (paste) into a bowl and mix together.

4 Heat the oil in a Balti pan or wok. Add the fish in batches so the pan is not crowded, and deep-fry for 3–4 minutes until golden brown. Transfer the fish on to paper towels to drain then keep warm in a low oven while you cook the rest of the fish.

5 Serve the fish hot with lemon wedges and the dip.

Spiced Chicken Koftas with Lime Pickle

SERVES 4

*500 g / 1lb skinned and boned chicken,
    chopped coarsely*
1 garlic clove
2.5 cm / 1 inch piece ginger root, grated
4 tsp garam masala (see page 22)
½ tsp ground turmeric
2 tbsp chopped fresh coriander (cilantro)
½ green (bell) pepper, chopped coarsely
2 fresh green chillies, deseeded
½ tsp salt
6 tbsp oil
1 jar lime pickle to serve
lime wedges to garnish

1 Put all the ingredients except the oil
and lime pickle into a food processor
or blender and process until the mixture
is chopped finely. Alternatively, finely
chop the chicken, garlic, ginger, (bell)
pepper and chillies, and mix together in a
bowl with the garam masala, turmeric,
coriander (cilantro) and salt.

2 Carefully shape the chicken mixture
into 16 small balls.

3 Heat the oil in a Balti pan or wok and
fry the koftas for 8–10 minutes,
turning them occasionally to ensure they
cook evenly. If you cannot fit all the
koftas into the pan at once, keep the first
batch warm in a low oven while you fry
the remaining koftas.

4 Drain the koftas on paper towels and
serve hot with lime pickle and a
garnish of lemon wedges.

VEGETARIAN KOFTAS

*You could make these into vegetarian
koftas by substituting 500 g / 1 lb of
mixed vegetables such as potatoes,
carrots or pumpkin for the chicken. Add
the vegetables in place of the chicken in
step 1, adding 1 egg to bind the
ingredients together.*

Balti Mushroom Paneer

SERVES 4

2 tbsp oil
2 small onions, sliced
2 tsp brown mustard seeds
1 garlic clove, crushed
2.5 cm / 1 inch piece ginger root, grated
½ tsp chilli powder
500 g / 1lb mixed mushrooms, such as
   oyster, shiitake, chestnut (crimini) and flat
125 g / 4 oz paneer (see right), cut into
   1 cm / ½ inch cubes
150 ml / ¼ pint / ⅔ cup Balti Sauce (see
   page 9) or chicken stock
¼ tsp salt
2 tsp garam masala (see page 22)
1 tbsp chopped fresh coriander (cilantro)

1 Heat the oil in a Balti pan or wok. Add the onions and mustard seeds and fry until the onions have softened.

2 Stir in the garlic, ginger and chilli powder and stir-fry for 1 minute.

3 Add the mushrooms and paneer and stir-fry for 2 minutes.

4 Stir in the Balti sauce or stock, the salt and garam masala and simmer for 5–7 minutes.

5 Stir in the chopped fresh coriander (cilantro) and serve.

PANEER

Paneer is the traditional homemade fresh cheese of Pakistan and India and is available in Asian stores. Tofu (bean curd) can be used as a substitute.

Paneer is very simple and quick to make. Bring to the boil 1.2 litres / 2 pints / 5 cups of milk, add 3 tablespoons of vinegar (any type) or lemon juice, and stir until the milk separates. Strain the curds through a clean piece of muslin (cheesecloth) or a tea towel (dish cloth). Flatten the paneer on to a plate and put a weighted plate on top to force out the liquid. Leave overnight. Use as required.

Minty Lamb Kebabs with Cucumber & Yogurt

SERVES 4

2 tsp coriander seeds
2 tsp cumin seeds
3 cloves
3 green cardamom pods
6 black peppercorns
1 cm / ½ inch piece ginger root
2 garlic cloves
2 tbsp chopped fresh mint
1 small onion, chopped
425 g / 14 oz / 1¾ cups minced (ground)
  lamb
½ tsp salt
lime slices to serve

DIP:
150 ml / 5 fl oz / ⅔ cup natural yogurt
2 tbsp chopped fresh mint
7 cm / 3 inch piece of cucumber, grated
1 tsp mango chutney

1 Dry-fry the coriander, cumin, cloves, cardamom pods and peppercorns until they turn a shade darker and release a roasted aroma.

2 Grind the roasted spices together in a coffee grinder, spice mill or pestle and mortar.

3 Put the ginger and garlic into a food processor or blender and process to a purée. Add the ground spices, mint, onion, lamb and salt and process until chopped finely. Alternatively, finely chop the garlic and ginger and mix with the ground spices and remaining kebab ingredients.

4 Mould the kebab mixture into small sausage shapes on 4 kebab skewers. Cook under a preheated hot grill (broiler) for 10–15 minutes, turning the skewers occasionally.

5 To make the cucumber and yogurt dip, mix all the ingredients together.

6 Serve the lamb kebabs with lime slices and the dip.

Traditional Balti Chicken

SERVES 4

3 tbsp oil
4 green cardamom pods
2 tsp cumin seeds
2 onions, sliced
2 garlic cloves, crushed
1.25 kg / 2½ lb chicken, skinned and jointed
    into 8 pieces, or 8 small chicken portions
1 tsp chilli powder
½ tsp salt
1 tsp garam masala (see right)
90 ml / 3½ fl oz / 6 tbsp water
10 tomatoes, chopped coarsely
2 tbsp chopped fresh coriander (cilantro)

1 Heat the oil in a Balti pan or wok, add the cardamom pods and cumin seeds and fry until the seeds pop.

2 Stir in the onions and garlic and fry until golden brown.

3 Add the chicken and stir-fry for 5–6 minutes until brown.

4 Stir in the chilli powder, salt, garam masala, water and tomatoes. Bring to the boil, then turn the heat down and

simmer for 20–25 minutes, until the chicken juices run clear when the thickest parts of the pieces are pierced with a sharp knife. Turn the chicken over halfway through cooking.

5 Stir in the coriander (cilantro) and serve at once.

GARAM MASALA

Ready-prepared garam masala can be bought in supermarkets and Asian food stores, but you may prefer to make your own. There are many variations in the recipe, and this one can be altered to suit your taste.

Roast 3 cm / 1¼ inch cinnamon stick, ¾ teaspoon black peppercorns, 8 green cardamom pods, 1 teaspoon cloves, 1 teaspoon cumin seeds, 1 teaspoon coriander seeds and ½ small nutmeg in a dry Balti pan or heavy frying pan (skillet) or in a preheated oven at 180°C / 350°F / Gas mark 4 until they turn a slightly darker colour. Leave to cool, then grind to a fine powder in a coffee grinder, spice mill or pestle and mortar.

Balti Chicken Paneer

SERVES 4

60 g / 2 oz / ½ cup ground almonds
250 g / 8 oz / 1 cup chopped tomatoes
2 fresh green chillies, chopped
1 tsp poppy seeds
1 garlic clove
150 ml / ¼ pint / ⅔ cup natural yogurt
90 g / 3 oz / ⅔ cup butter
750 g / 1½ lb chicken breast meat, cut into
    2.5 cm / 1 inch cubes
175 g / 6 oz paneer (see page 18), cut into
    1 cm / ½ inch cubes
1 tsp ground cumin
1 tsp paprika
1 tsp garam masala (see page 22)
¼ tsp ground cinnamon
½ tsp salt

TO GARNISH:
1 tbsp chopped fresh coriander (cilantro)
30 g / 1 oz / ¼ cup flaked (slivered) almonds,
    toasted

1 Put the ground almonds, tomatoes, chillies, poppy seeds and garlic in a food processor or blender and blend to a smooth paste. Alternatively, push the tomatoes through a sieve (strainer), finely chop the chillies and garlic, crush the poppy seeds, then mix together the tomatoes, chillies, garlic, poppy seeds and ground almonds. Stir the yogurt into the tomato mixture.

2 Heat the butter in a Balti pan or wok, add the cubes of chicken and stir-fry for 5 minutes.

3 Add the paneer, cumin, paprika, garam masala, cinnamon and salt and stir-fry for 1 minute.

4 Add the tomato and yogurt mixture slowly to prevent the yogurt curdling. Simmer for 10–15 minutes until the chicken juices run clear when the chicken is pierced with a sharp knife.

5 Serve garnished with the fresh coriander (cilantro) and flaked (slivered) almonds.

Chicken & Black-eye Beans (Peas)

SERVES 4

250 g / 8 oz / 1 generous cup dried black-eye beans (peas), soaked overnight and drained

1 tsp salt

2 onions, chopped

2 garlic cloves, crushed

1 tsp ground turmeric

1 tsp ground cumin

1.25 kg / 2½ lb chicken, jointed into 8 pieces

1 green (bell) pepper, chopped

2 tbsp oil

2.5 cm / 1 inch piece ginger root, grated

2 tsp coriander seeds

½ tsp fennel seeds

2 tsp garam masala (see page 22)

1 tbsp chopped fresh coriander (cilantro) to garnish

1 Put the beans into a Balti pan, wok or saucepan with the salt, onions, garlic, turmeric and cumin. Cover with water, bring to the boil and cook for 15 minutes.

2 Add the chicken and green (bell) pepper to the pan and bring to the boil. Lower the heat and simmer gently for 30 minutes until the beans are tender and the chicken juices run clear when the thickest parts of the pieces are pierced with a sharp knife.

3 Heat the oil in a Balti pan, wok or frying pan (skillet) and fry the ginger, coriander seeds and fennel seeds for 30 seconds.

4 Stir the ginger, coriander seeds and fennel seeds into the chicken and add the garam masala. Simmer for a further 5 minutes and serve garnished with fresh coriander (cilantro).

CANNED BEANS

For convenience, you can use 425 g / 14 oz can of black-eye beans (peas) instead of dried beans (peas). Add at step 2.

Balti Quail

SERVES 4

4 quail, roughly jointed
1.5 cm / ⅔ inch piece ginger root, grated
2 garlic cloves, crushed
1 tsp ground cumin
2 tsp garam masala (see page 22)
2 tsp paprika
1 tsp ground turmeric
1 tbsp chopped fresh mint
⅔ tsp salt
250 ml / 8 fl oz / 1 cup natural yogurt
2 tbsp oil
8 baby onions, total weight about
    250 g / 8 oz
4 courgettes (zucchini), sliced thickly
1 fresh green chilli, chopped
4 lime wedges to garnish

1 Using a sharp knife, make cuts in several places in the skin and flesh of each quail joint.

2 Mix together the ginger, garlic, cumin, garam masala, paprika, turmeric, mint, salt and yogurt. Add the quail and coat in the sauce.

3 Cover and leave in the refrigerator to marinate for 2 hours or overnight.

4 Put the quail on a rack over a roasting tin (pan) containing approximately 2.5 cm/1 inch depth of water; this keeps the quail moist during cooking. Roast the quail in a preheated oven at 200°C/400°F/ Gas mark 6 for 30 minutes, until the quail juices run clear when the thickest part of each piece is pierced with a sharp knife.

5 Heat the oil in a Balti pan or wok and fry the onions, courgettes (zucchini) and chilli for 5–6 minutes until golden brown and tender.

6 Add the cooked quail to the onion mixture and serve garnished with lime wedges.

VARIATION

Baby chicken or chicken joints can be used for this dish instead of quail.

Sweet & Sour Balti Duck

SERVES 4

4 tbsp oil
½ tsp cumin seeds
½ tsp brown mustard seeds
½ tsp crushed dried pomegranate seeds
1 onion, sliced
1 garlic clove, chopped
1 cm / ½ inch piece ginger root, shredded
2 fresh green chillies, sliced
4 duck breasts, boned and sliced into
    5 cm / 2 inch strips
½ tsp salt
150 ml / ¼ pint / ⅔ cup orange juice
1 orange, quartered and sliced
2 tsp ground turmeric
½ tsp garam masala (see page 22)
1 tbsp white wine vinegar
shredded orange rind to garnish

1 Heat the oil in a Balti pan or wok and fry the cumin seeds, mustard seeds and pomegranate seeds until they start popping.

2 Add the onion, garlic, ginger and chillies and stir-fry until the onions are golden brown.

3 Add the duck and stir-fry for 5 minutes until it is brown on both sides.

4 Stir in the salt, orange juice, orange slices, turmeric, garam masala and vinegar and bring to the boil. Lower the heat and simmer for 15–20 minutes until the duck is tender but still pinkish inside; if you prefer duck to be well done, cook for longer. Serve garnished with shredded orange rind.

POMEGRANATE SEEDS

Dried pomegranate seeds can be bought at Asian stores and will give a very individual tangy taste. Alternatively, you could use the seeds from the fresh fruit.

Pathan Beef Stir-fry

SERVES 4

750 g / 1½ lb fillet of beef, cut into
  2.5 cm / 1 inch strips
2 tbsp oil
1 onion, sliced
2.5 cm / 1 inch piece ginger root, cut into
  strips
1 fresh red chilli, deseeded and sliced
2 carrots, cut into strips
1 green (bell) pepper, cut into strips
1 tsp garam masala (see page 22)
1 tbsp toasted sesame seeds

MARINADE:
1 tsp dried fenugreek
1 tsp brown mustard seeds, ground
1 tsp ground cinnamon
1 tsp ground cumin
1 garlic clove, crushed
150 ml / ¼ pint / ⅔ cup natural yogurt

1 To make the marinade, mix all the
marinade ingredients in a bowl.

2 Add the beef to the marinade, stir to
coat, then cover and leave to
marinate for 1–2 hours, or overnight in
the refrigerator.

3 Heat the oil in a Balti pan or wok, add
the onion and stir-fry until softened.

4 Stir in the ginger, chilli, carrots and
green (bell) pepper and stir-fry for
1 minute. Add the garam masala and beef
with the marinade liquids, and stir-fry for
8–10 minutes until the beef is tender; it is
best if it is still pinkish inside.

5 Stir in the toasted sesame seeds and
serve immediately.

Tamarind Beef Balti

Serves 4

125 g / 4 oz tamarind block, broken into
   pieces
150 ml / ¼ pint / ⅔ cup water
2 tbsp tomato purée (paste)
1 tbsp granulated sugar
2.5 cm / 1 inch piece ginger root, chopped
1 garlic clove, chopped
½ tsp salt
1 onion, chopped
2 tbsp oil
1 tsp cumin seeds
1 tsp coriander seeds
1 tsp brown mustard seeds
4 curry leaves
750 g / 1½ lb braising steak, cut into
   2.5 cm / 1 inch cubes and par-cooked
   (see page 9)
1 red (bell) pepper, cut in half and sliced
2 fresh green chillies, deseeded and sliced
1 tsp garam masala (see page 22)
1 tbsp chopped fresh coriander (cilantro)
   to garnish

1 Soak the tamarind overnight in the
water. Strain the soaked tamarind,
keeping the liquid.

2 Put the tamarind, tomato purée
(paste), sugar, ginger, garlic, salt and
onion into a food processor or blender
and mix to a smooth purée. Alternatively,
mash the ingredients together in a bowl.

3 Heat the oil in a Balti pan or wok, add
the cumin seeds, coriander seeds,
mustard seeds and curry leaves, and cook
until the spices start popping.

4 Stir the par-cooked beef into the
spices and stir-fry for 2–4 minutes
until the meat is browned.

5 Add the red (bell) pepper, chillies,
garam masala, tamarind mixture and
reserved tamarind liquid and cook for
20–25 minutes. Serve garnished with
fresh coriander (cilantro).

SUBSTITUTES

*Bay leaves can be substituted for the
curry leaves, although they will not give
quite the same spicy taste. Instead of
tamarind you could use 4 tablespoons of
lemon juice.*

Lamb Koftas with Spinach & Cardamom

SERVES 4

5 tbsp oil
2 tsp cardamom seeds
6 black peppercorns, crushed
1 tsp cumin seeds
1 onion, chopped finely
1 garlic clove, crushed
150 ml / ¼ pint / ⅔ cup natural yogurt
500 g / 1 lb chopped fresh spinach
½ tsp grated nutmeg
1 tsp garam masala (see page 22)
1 tsp salt
90 g / 3 oz / ¾ cup split almonds, shredded

KOFTAS:
1 onion, quartered
1 garlic clove
1 fresh green chilli, deseeded
1 tsp garam masala (see page 22)
1 tsp salt
750 g / 1½ lb / 3 cups minced (ground) lamb

1 To make the koftas, put the onion, garlic and chilli into a food processor or blender and process until chopped finely. Add the garam masala, salt and lamb and process to combine the ingredients. Alternatively, finely chop the onion, garlic and chilli, then mix with the garam masala, salt and lamb in a bowl.

2 Shape the lamb mixture into small balls. Heat 3 tablespoons of the oil in a Balti pan or wok, add the koftas in batches and cook, turning frequently, until evenly browned. Remove the koftas from the pan with a slotted spoon, drain on paper towels and keep warm.

3 Heat the remaining oil in the pan and fry the cardamom seeds, peppercorns and cumin seeds until they start popping. Add the onion and garlic and cook until golden brown.

4 Gradually add the yogurt, stirring all the time to prevent it curdling. Stir in the spinach, nutmeg, garam masala, salt, two-thirds of the almonds and the koftas and simmer for 30 minutes. Sprinkle over the remaining almonds and serve.

Balti Lamb Rogan Josh

SERVES 4

3 tbsp fennel seeds
1 cm / ½ inch piece cinnamon stick
4 black peppercorns
3 tbsp oil
2 onions, sliced
2 garlic cloves, crushed
2.5 cm / 1 inch piece ginger root, grated
750 g / 1½ lb lamb, cut into 2.5 cm / 1 inch
   cubes and par-cooked (see page 9)
8 tomatoes, chopped
1 green (bell) pepper, sliced
150 ml / ¼ pint / ⅔ cup natural yogurt
3 tsp paprika
½ tsp chilli powder
½ tsp garam masala (see page 22)
300 ml / ½ pint / 1¼ cups Balti Sauce (see
   page 9) or lamb stock

TO GARNISH :
2 tbsp chopped fresh coriander (cilantro)
2 tbsp natural yogurt

1 Grind the fennel seeds, cinnamon
stick and peppercorns to a fine
powder in a coffee grinder, spice mill or
pestle and mortar.

2 Heat the oil in a Balti pan or wok, add
the onions and stir-fry until softened.
Add the garlic and ginger and stir-fry for
1 minute.

3 Add the par-cooked lamb, stir-fry for
3 minutes, then add the tomatoes and
green (bell) pepper. Stir-fry for 1 minute.

4 Slowly stir in the yogurt, then add the
paprika, chilli powder, ground spices,
garam masala and Balti sauce or lamb
stock. Simmer for 30 minutes until the
sauce is reduced to the consistency of a
thick gravy.

5 Serve garnished with fresh coriander
(cilantro) and yogurt.

Masala Lamb & Lentils

SERVES 4

2 tbsp oil
1 tsp cumin seeds
2 bay leaves
2.5 cm / 1 inch piece cinnamon stick
1 onion, chopped
750 g / 1½ lb lean, boneless lamb, cut into
    2.5 cm / 1 inch cubes
125 g / 4 oz / ½ cup split yellow lentils,
    soaked for 6 hours and drained
1 tsp salt
1 fresh green chilli, sliced
1.25 litres / 2¼ pints / 5 cups water
1 garlic clove, crushed
¼ tsp ground turmeric
1 tsp chilli powder
½ tsp garam masala (see page 22)
    (optional)
1 tbsp chopped fresh coriander (cilantro)
    (optional)

1 Heat the oil in a Balti pan or wok and
  add the cumin seeds, bay leaves and
cinnamon stick and fry until the seeds
start popping.

2 Add the onion to the pan and stir-fry
  until golden brown.

3 Stir the lamb into the onion and stir-
  fry until browned.

4 Add the lentils, salt, chilli, water, garlic,
  turmeric and chilli powder. Bring to
the boil, then simmer for 1 hour until the
meat and lentils are tender.

5 Taste for seasoning and stir the garam
  masala into the pan if liked, and cook
for a further 5 minutes. Stir in the
coriander (cilantro), if using, and serve.

TIMESAVER

*To save time on soaking, use a 425 g /
14 oz can of lentils. These should be
added at the end of step 4 and cooked
for 15 minutes. The meat still needs the
same cooking time.*

Balti Keema with Sweet Potatoes, Okra & Spinach

SERVES 4

250 g / 8 oz sweet potatoes, cut into chunks
175 g / 6 oz okra
2 tbsp oil
2 onions, sliced
2 garlic cloves, crushed
1 cm / ½ inch piece ginger root, chopped
500 g / 1 lb / 2 cups minced (ground) lamb
250 g / 8 oz / 6 cups fresh spinach,
    chopped
300 ml / ½ pint / 1¼ cups lamb stock
½ tsp salt
125 g / 4 oz / 1 cup pine nuts
125 g / 4 oz / ¾ cup sultanas (golden
    raisins)
1 tbsp granulated sugar
3 tsp garam masala (see page 22)
rice or naan bread to serve

1 Bring 2 saucepans of water to the boil.
Add the sweet potatoes to one and
the okra to the other. Boil both vegetables
for 4–5 minutes, then drain well. Cut the
okra into 1 cm/ ½ inch slices. Set aside
both vegetables.

2 Heat the oil in a Balti pan or wok, add
the onions and stir-fry until golden
brown. Stir in the garlic and ginger and fry
for 1 minute.

3 Add the lamb to the pan and stir-fry
for 5 minutes.

4 Stir in the sweet potato, okra and
spinach and stir-fry for 2 minutes.

5 Add the stock, salt, pine nuts, sultanas
(golden raisins), sugar and garam
masala and simmer for 10–15 minutes
until the sauce has thickened. Serve with
rice or naan bread.

ALTERNATIVES

*Sweet potato gives a wonderful flavour to
the dish, but you could use pumpkin,
which has a sweetish taste similar to that
of sweet potatoes, or ordinary potatoes.*

Balti Scallops with Coriander (Cilantro) & Tomato

SERVES 4

750 g / 1½ lb shelled scallops
2 tbsp oil
2 onions, chopped
3 tomatoes, quartered
2 fresh green chillies, sliced
4 lime wedges to garnish

MARINADE:
3 tbsp chopped fresh coriander (cilantro)
2.5 cm / 1 inch piece ginger root, grated
1 tsp ground coriander
3 tbsp lemon juice
grated rind of 1 lemon
¼ tsp ground black pepper
½ tsp salt
½ tsp ground cumin
1 garlic clove, crushed

1 To make the marinade, mix all the ingredients together in a bowl.

2 Put the scallops into a bowl. Add the marinade and turn the scallops until they are well coated. Then cover and leave to marinate for 1 hour or overnight in the refrigerator.

3 Heat the oil in a Balti pan or wok, add the onions and stir-fry until softened. Add the tomatoes and chillies and stir-fry for 1 minute.

4 Add the scallops and stir-fry for 6–8 minutes until the scallops are cooked through, but still succulent inside. Serve garnished with lime wedges.

SCALLOPS

It is best to buy the scallops fresh in the shell with the roe – you will need 1.5 kg / 3 lb. The fishmonger will clean them and remove the shell for you.

Tiger Prawns (Jumbo Shrimp) with Spiced Courgettes (Zucchini)

SERVES 4

3 tbsp oil
2 onions, chopped
3 garlic cloves, chopped
1 cm / ½ inch piece ginger root, chopped
250 g / 8 oz courgettes (zucchini), sliced
1 tsp dried pomegranate seeds, crushed
8 tomatoes, chopped
1 tbsp tomato purée (paste)
150 ml / ¼ pint / ⅔ cup coconut milk
2 tbsp chopped fresh coriander (cilantro)
1 tsp chilli powder
1 tsp ground cumin
½ tsp salt
500 g / 1 lb peeled cooked tiger prawns
    (jumbo shrimp)
fresh coriander (cilantro) to garnish

1 Heat the oil in a Balti pan or wok, add the onions and stir-fry until golden brown. Add the garlic and ginger and stir-fry for 1 minute.

2 Stir the courgettes (zucchini) and pomegranate seeds into the pan and stir-fry for 2 minutes.

3 Add the tomatoes, tomato purée (paste), coconut milk, fresh coriander (cilantro), chilli powder, cumin and salt and stir-fry for a further 2 minutes.

4 Stir in the prawns (shrimp), bring to the boil then simmer for 6 minutes. Serve garnished with fresh coriander (cilantro).

VARIATION

This recipe also works well with lobster, monkfish or scallops instead of tiger prawns (jumbo shrimp). Scallops and lobster should be cooked for only 3 minutes.

Balti Cod & Red Lentils

SERVES 4

2 tbsp oil
¼ tsp ground asafoetida (optional)
1 tbsp crushed aniseed
1 tsp ground ginger
1 tsp chilli powder
¼ tsp ground turmeric
250 g / 8 oz / 1 cup split red lentils, washed
1 tsp salt
500 g / 1 lb cod, skinned, filleted and cut
    into 2.5 cm / 1 inch cubes
1 fresh red chilli, chopped
3 tbsp natural yogurt
2 tbsp chopped fresh coriander (cilantro)

1 Heat the oil in a Balti pan or wok, add the asafoetida, if using, and fry for about 10 seconds to burn off the smell of the asafoetida. Add the aniseed, ginger, chilli powder and turmeric and fry for 30 seconds.

2 Stir in the lentils and salt and add enough water to cover the lentils. Bring to the boil, then simmer gently for 45 minutes, until the lentils are soft but not mushy.

3 Add the cod and fresh chilli, bring to the boil and simmer for a further 10 minutes.

4 Stir in the yogurt and fresh coriander (cilantro) and serve straight away.

ASAFOETIDA

Asafoetida is a digestive, so it will help in the digestion of the lentils. Ground asafoetida is easier to use than the type that comes in a block. It should only be used in small quantities. Do not be put off by the smell, which is very pungent.

Creamy Fish & Prawn (Shrimp) Masala

SERVES 4

1 tsp ground coriander
250 ml / 8 fl oz / 1 cup natural yogurt
1 tsp ground turmeric
1 tsp salt
500 g / 1 lb firm white fish such as cod or
    haddock, skinned, filleted and cut into
    2.5 cm / 1 inch cubes
250 g / 8 oz / ¼ cup peeled cooked tiger
    prawns (jumbo shrimp)
2 tbsp oil
1 tsp brown mustard seeds
1 onion, chopped
1 garlic clove, crushed
2 tsp garam masala (see page 22)
2 tbsp chopped fresh coriander (cilantro)
120 ml / 4 fl oz / ½ cup double (heavy)
    cream

TO GARNISH:
1 tbsp crushed dried red chillies
sprigs of fresh coriander (cilantro)

1 Put the ground coriander, yogurt, turmeric and salt into a bowl and stir together. Add the fish and prawns (shrimp) and leave to marinate for 1 hour.

2 Heat the oil in a Balti pan or wok, add the mustard seeds and fry until they start popping.

3 Add the onion to the pan, stir-fry until golden brown, then add the garlic and stir-fry for 1 minute.

4 Stir in the garam masala, fresh coriander (cilantro) and marinated fish and prawns (shrimp). Simmer for 10–15 minutes until the fish flakes easily when tested with a fork. Stir in the cream during the last few minutes of cooking.

5 Serve garnished with crushed dried red chillies and sprigs of fresh coriander (cilantro).

Monkfish & Okra Balti

750 g / 1½ lb monkfish, cut into
   3 cm / 1¼ inch cubes
250 g / 8 oz okra
2 tbsp oil
1 onion, sliced
1 garlic clove, crushed
2.5 cm / 1 inch piece ginger root, sliced
150 ml / ¼ pint / ⅔ cup coconut milk or
   fish stock
2 tsp garam masala (see page 22)

MARINADE:
3 tbsp lemon juice
grated rind of 1 lemon
¼ tsp aniseed
½ tsp salt
½ tsp ground black pepper

TO GARNISH:
4 lime wedges
sprigs of fresh coriander (cilantro)

1 To make the marinade, mix the ingredients together in a bowl.

2 Stir the monkfish into the bowl and leave to marinate for 1 hour.

3 Bring a large saucepan of water to the boil, add the okra and boil for 4–5 minutes. Drain well and cut into 1 cm/ ½ inch slices.

4 Heat the oil in a Balti pan or wok, add the onion and stir-fry until golden brown. Add the garlic and ginger and fry for 1 minute.

5 Add the fish and marinade juices to the pan and stir-fry for 2 minutes.

6 Stir in the okra, coconut milk or stock and garam masala and simmer for 10 minutes. Serve garnished with lime wedges and fresh coriander (cilantro).

Sweet Potatoes & Spinach

SERVES 4

*500 g / 1lb sweet potatoes, cut into
    2.5 cm / 1 inch cubes*
4 tbsp oil
2 onions, sliced
1 garlic clove, crushed
125 g / 4 oz / 1 cup pine nuts, toasted
500 g / 1 lb fresh spinach
1 tsp garam masala (see page 22)
2 tsp chopped dried red chillies
2 tbsp water
freshly grated nutmeg to serve

1 Boil the sweet potatoes in salted water for 5 minutes until half cooked. Drain and set aside.

2 Heat the oil in a Balti pan or wok, add the onions and stir-fry until golden brown.

3 Add the garlic, sweet potatoes and pine nuts to the pan and stir-fry for 2 minutes until the sweet potatoes have absorbed the oil.

4 Stir in the spinach, garam masala and dried chillies and stir-fry for 2 minutes. Add the water and stir-fry for 4 minutes until the sweet potatoes and spinach are tender.

5 Serve with freshly grated nutmeg sprinkled over.

SUBSTITUTES

You can substitute 1kg / 2 lb of frozen leaf spinach for the fresh spinach. Fresh chillies can be used instead of dried chillies.

Mixed Vegetable Balti

SERVES 4

250 g / 8 oz / 1 cup split yellow peas,
   washed
3 tbsp oil
1 tsp onion seeds
2 onions, sliced
125 g / 4 oz courgettes (zucchini), sliced
125 g / 4 oz potatoes, cut into
   1 cm / ½ inch cubes
125 g / 4 oz carrots, sliced
1 small aubergine (eggplant), sliced
250 g / 8 oz tomatoes, chopped
300 ml / ½ pint / 1¼ cups water
3 garlic cloves, chopped
1 tsp ground cumin
1 tsp ground coriander
1 tsp salt
2 fresh green chillies, sliced
½ tsp garam masala (see page 22)
2 tbsp chopped fresh coriander (cilantro)

1 Put the split peas into a saucepan and
cover with salted water. Bring to the
boil and simmer for 30 minutes. Drain the
peas and keep warm.

2 Heat the oil in a Balti pan or wok, add
the onion seeds and fry until they
start popping. Add the onions and stir-fry
until golden brown.

3 Add the courgettes (zucchini),
potatoes, carrots and aubergine
(eggplant) to the pan and stir-fry for
2 minutes.

4 Stir in the tomatoes, water, garlic,
cumin, ground coriander, salt, chillies,
garam masala and reserved split peas.
Bring to the boil, then simmer for 15
minutes until all the vegetables are tender.
Stir the fresh coriander (cilantro) into the
vegetables and serve.

Balti Dal

SERVES 4

250 g / 8 oz / 1 cup chang dal or split
    yellow peas, washed
½ tsp ground turmeric
1 tsp ground coriander
1 tsp salt
4 curry leaves
2 tbsp oil
½ tsp ground asafoetida (optional)
1 tsp cumin seeds
2 onions, chopped
2 garlic cloves, crushed
1 cm / ½ inch piece ginger root, grated
½ tsp garam masala (see page 22)

1 Put the chang dal in a saucepan and pour in enough water to cover by 2.5 cm / 1 inch. Bring to the boil and spoon off the scum that has formed.

2 Add the turmeric, ground coriander, salt and curry leaves and simmer for 1 hour. The chang dal should be tender but not mushy.

3 Heat the oil in a Balti pan or wok, add the asafoetida, if using, and fry for 30 seconds. Add the cumin seeds and fry until they start popping. Add the onions and stir-fry until golden brown.

4 Add the garlic, ginger, garam masala and chang dal and stir-fry for 2 minutes. Serve hot with a Balti curry.

Pumpkin Korma

SERVES 4

4 tbsp oil
½ tsp onion seeds
4 curry leaves
2 onions, chopped
500 g / 1 lb peeled and deseeded pumpkin,
    cut into 2.5 cm / 1 inch cubes
150 ml / ¼ pint / ⅔ cup natural yogurt
1 cm / ½ inch piece ginger root, grated
2 garlic cloves, crushed
125 g / 4 oz / 1 cup ground almonds
½ tsp ground turmeric
½ tsp chilli powder
½ tsp garam masala (see page 22)
1 tsp salt
150 ml / ¼ pint / ⅔ cup coconut milk
1 tbsp chopped fresh coriander (cilantro)

TO GARNISH:
1 tbsp chopped toasted almonds
1 tbsp chopped fresh coriander (cilantro)

1 Heat the oil in a Balti pan or wok, add the onion seeds and curry leaves and fry until the seeds start popping.

2 Add the onions to the pan and stir-fry until golden brown.

3 Stir in the pumpkin and stir-fry until golden brown.

4 Stir in the yogurt gradually to prevent it curdling. Add the ginger, garlic, almonds, turmeric, chilli powder, garam masala, salt, coconut milk and fresh coriander (cilantro) and simmer for 10–15 minutes until the pumpkin is tender. Serve garnished with toasted almonds and fresh coriander (cilantro).

Aromatic Basmati Rice & Spicy Saffron Rice

AROMATIC BASMATI RICE

1 tbsp oil
1 cinnamon stick
2 dried bay leaves
4 green cardamom pods
4 black peppercorns
250 g / 8 oz / 1 cup basmati rice, washed
  and soaked
1 tsp salt

1 Heat the oil in a heavy-based saucepan and fry the cinnamon, bay leaves, cardamom pods and black peppercorns for 30 seconds.

2 Add the rice and salt and enough water to cover the rice by 2.5 cm/ 1 inch. Cover with a tight-fitting lid, bring to the boil and simmer for 20 minutes or until all the water has been absorbed and the rice is tender.

SPICY SAFFRON RICE

60 g / 2 oz / ¼ cup butter or ghee
1 onion, chopped
½ tsp saffron strands
1 tsp cumin seeds
250 g / 8 oz / 1 cup basmati rice, washed
  and soaked
1 tsp salt
90 g / 3 oz / ⅔ cup split almonds, cut in
  slivers and toasted

1 Heat the butter or ghee in a heavy-based saucepan, add the onion and stir-fry. Add the saffron strands and cumin seeds and fry for 30 seconds.

2 Add the rice and fry for 2 minutes until it has absorbed the oil and the saffron colour. Add the salt and enough water to cover the rice by 2.5 cm/1 inch. Cover with a tight-fitting lid and simmer for 20 minutes until all the water has been absorbed and the rice is tender. Stir in the toasted almonds.

Index